The Little Schoolhouse in the Woods

Landon the Squirrel

Copyright © *Kellie Bahri,* 2024

All Rights Reserved

This book is subject to the condition that no part of this book is to be reproduced, transmitted in any form or means; electronic or mechanical, stored in a retrieval system, photocopied, recorded, scanned, or otherwise. Any of these actions require the proper written permission of the author.

ISBN: 979-8-218-47612-0

For anyone who needs to be reminded that
your uniqueness is your superpower.
You were created for greatness. SHINE!

Ring! Ring! Ring! The school bell rang.

Landon was running across the school yard, his papers flying out behind him. He was in a hurry and forgot to zip up his backpack.

"Hurry, Landon," Beaver said waving to his friend.

"You're always late," Bear growled.

The day had just begun and Landon was already feeling frustrated.

During the Pledge of Allegiance, Landon excitedly stood on his desk because he knew all the words.

"I pledge allegiance," Landon yelled proudly.

"Shhh, Landon," Beaver whispered trying to keep his friend from getting into trouble.

Ms. Hawks asked everyone to write a story, but Landon couldn't think of the perfect words, so he did a lot of erasing, and it made a hole in his paper.

To fix his paper, he asked his friend, Fox, for a piece of tape, but when Landon pulled it, the tape wrapped all around him until he couldn't move.

"Landon, you look like a mummy," Fox said.

Quiet reading was the hardest for Landon. He couldn't focus on his book, and he wanted to tell Mouse about his big day after school.

He tried to get Mouse's attention, but that didn't work out so well.

She told Ms. Hawks, "Landon isn't reading and he keeps poking me," squeaked Mouse.

Later, Landon was so focused on his cars that he didn't hear Ms. Hawks ask him to get in line for lunch, and everyone had to wait for him to get ready. Landon was embarrassed.

Ms. Hawks noticed Landon looking a little sad.

"Landon, would you like to have lunch with me?" whispered Ms. Hawks.

Looking up slowly, Landon nodded yes.

"Landon, my little squirrel, what's wrong?" she asked with a tender voice.

Landon looked up, "I try hard to do things the right way, but I always mess up," he said with a sniffle.

"Come sit down. I have something to share with you," Ms. Hawks said.

"Landon, we all have special gifts and you have lots of gifts that the world needs," Ms. Hawks said, hugging Landon.

"We are all different in our classroom and each of us has different strengths. This is what makes each of us very special."

With a warm smile, Ms. Hawks said, "I would like to tell you about the strengths I see in you."

Landon looked up and wiped away his tears and listened as hard as he could.

You are creative.

You are a problem solver.

You stay calm in times of trouble.

You focus on things you enjoy.

You are adventurous!

With each strength that Ms. Hawks shared, Landon smiled and began to feel proud of himself.

"The world needs your talents, Landon. You will change the world with your kind heart and your special gifts," Ms. Hawks said smiling.

"Landon, let's find some ways for you to feel confident in the classroom," Ms. Hawks said excitedly.

Landon felt a little embarrassed talking about the things he needed, but he knew Ms. Hawks was there to help him.

"Sometimes I don't know what to do with my hands… they don't like being still," Landon whispered to Ms. Hawks.

The first thing Landon thought to help would be having a few fidget toys to use while he worked so he could focus, instead of poking his friends.

"I really like stories, but reading is hard for me. I always have to think hard how to say the words and then I get confused. But, I like when you read to me because I can picture the story in my head."

Ms. Hawks thought listening to books would help Landon. He could enjoy hearing and following along with the stories, instead of becoming frustrated.

They also thought a special signal would help Landon know when he needed to slow down a little.

And lastly, they both agreed that having breaks to walk around and work out some energy would help. Landon could help do little errands for Ms. Hawks!

Landon felt proud to be a helper.

After talking with Ms. Hawks at lunch, Landon saw himself and his friends in a whole new way! He knew everyone had their own special gifts and being different made them special. He was ready to use his strengths to change the world...

...and so can YOU!

Kellie Bahri is a teacher, mother, and author in Michigan. Little School in the Woods was inspired by her son's experience in school having ADHD. She witnessed her son's self-esteem drop as he compared himself to others around him. While never quite fitting in at school, he excelled in creativity and kindness. As a teacher, Kellie makes certain that every child hears of their gifts and is reminded they are created for greatness. Encouraging children to not compare themselves to those around them, but rather to look inside and let their strengths shine.

Noella Bickel is an artist and educator based in the San Francisco Bay Area. Beginning art instruction at the age of ten, she knew early on that she loved animation and wanted to create her own films. She attended the School of Film and Television at Loyola Marymount University with a Bachelor of Arts in Animation in 2002. While she loved animation and art, she also found a passion for education. She earned multiple credentials and worked as a teacher since 2005. Currently, she teaches 8th grade US History and Leadership.

www.ingramcontent.com/pod-product-compliance
Lightning Source LLC
Chambersburg PA
CBRC091724070526
44585CB00008B/161